# The Crafty Art Book

## Jane Bull

Dorling Kindersley

LONDON, NEW YORK, MUNICH,
MELBOURNE, AND DELHI

DESIGN • Jane Bull
TEXT • Penelope Arlon
PHOTOGRAPHY • Andy Crawford
DESIGN ASSISTANCE • Sadie Thomas

PUBLISHING MANAGER • Sue Leonard
MANAGING ART EDITOR • Clare Shedden
PRODUCTION • Shivani Pandey
DTP DESIGNER • Almudena Díaz

For Charlotte, Billy, and James

First published in Great Britain in 2004 by
Dorling Kindersley Limited
80 Strand, London WC2R 0RL

A Penguin Company

2 4 6 8 10 9 7 5 3 1

A CIP catalogue record for this book
is available from the British Library

ISBN: 1-4053-0384-0

Colour reproduction by
GRB Editrice S.r.l., Verona, Italy
Printed and bound in China by Toppan

discover more at
**www.dk.com**

Get crafty
with your art

# A crafty book of arty ideas . . .

## to make perfect gifts...

## for family and friends

Ha Ha

# Crafty kit • Here's a guide to the materials

## Paper or card?

TRACING PAPER • You will need tracing paper for the Pirate Pete templates, although grease-proof paper is a good alternative.

TISSUE PAPER • Tissue paper is the best choice for the roses.

PAPER • Any thin paper can be used for the marble and other printing techniques.

CARD • Folded boxes can be made with paper or very thin card, paper is much easier to fold and surprisingly sturdy. Thin card is best for woolly web bases and for home-made cards and tags.

*Tissue paper*

## Paints and pens

POSTER PAINT • Is a very good all-round paint for paper and card. It is cheap and easy to use. When you are printing paper, use poster paint.

OIL PAINT • To make marble paper, you will need oil paints and turpentine – ask your parents to help you with this project.

FABRIC PENS • When you use fabric pens (to decorate Pirate Pete for example), follow the instructions on the packet to ensure the best results.

*Poster paint*

## Bits and bobs

To finish off your projects nicely, you will often need bits and bobs or odd household items. Keep your eyes open for things you can use in your arty crafts, such as:

- buttons and beads
- ribbon
- old paper
- anything with a texture that would work well for printing, like empty cotton reels, used-up pens, and old sponges.

☆ **Ask an adult.** You will see this sign if you need to ask an adult to help you.

*Scissors*

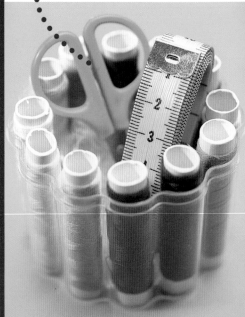

4

**used to make the projects in this book.**

## Pins and needles

WOOL • For knitting, woolly webs, and cross-stitch, you will need wool, which you buy in balls.

DARNING NEEDLE • If you are sewing with wool, you will need a darning needle, which has a big hole, or "eye".

KNITTING NEEDLES • Come in different sizes. In this book they are 4 mm (no. 8).

SEWING NEEDLE • For sewing with thin thread, you will need a sewing needle with a small eye – not a darning needle. If you have trouble threading a needle, you can buy a simple, cheap tool to make it easier.

PINS • Always pin material before you sew it.

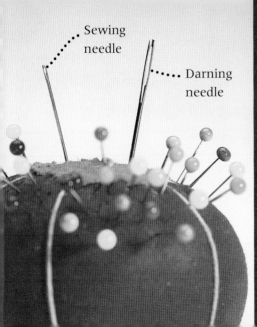

Sewing needle

Darning needle

## Backstitch

This quick, strong stitch is a bit like a doubled-up running stitch. When you use it to sew Pirate Pete, it will stop his filling from falling out.

Knot the end of the thread. Push the needle down and up through the fabric.

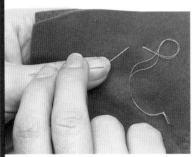

Pull the needle all the way through to the knot.

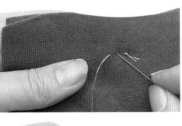

Put the needle between the knot and the dangling thread.

Bring the needle up ahead of the dangling thread.

Repeat these steps and sew over a few stitches to finish off.

## Fabrics

EMBROIDERY FABRIC • In order to make the cross-stitch patterns, you will have to buy special fabric called BINCA. It has big holes that you can easily put wool through.

COTTON FABRIC • For Pirate Pete and friends, white cotton is the best material. Old sheets and pillowcases would be perfect.

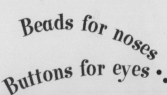

*Beads for noses*

*Buttons for eyes*

# Woolly webs

**Get yourself caught up** in
these woolly webs. When
you've got the knack, try
different shapes, different colours,
and different sizes – they're endless!

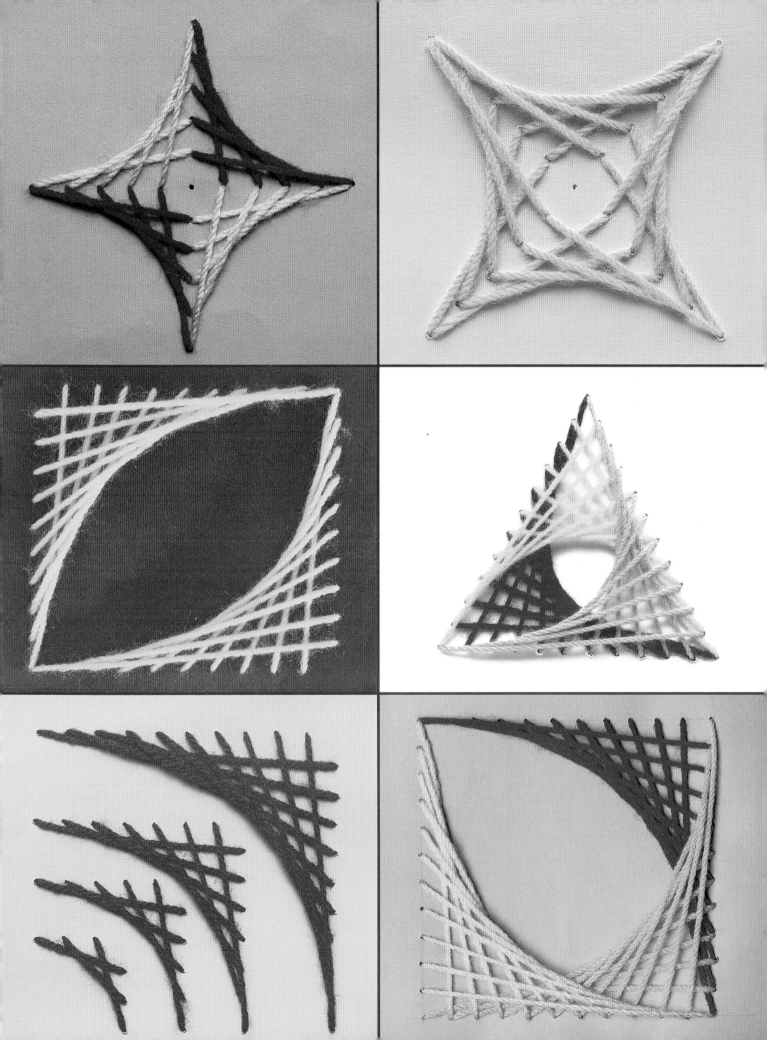

# WEAVING KIT

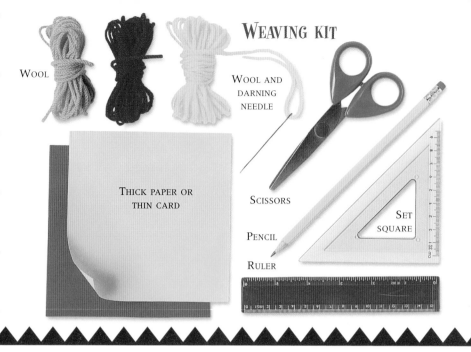

WOOL

WOOL AND DARNING NEEDLE

THICK PAPER OR THIN CARD

SCISSORS

PENCIL

RULER

SET SQUARE

Draw a right angle on your card of 10 cm by 10 cm (5 in by 5 in).

## 1 Draw a right angle

# Weaving tips

- Use thick paper or thin card. If the paper is too thin it will rip when you pull the thread through.
- For large patterns use wool, but for smaller designs lighter thread is best.
- When you get the hang of it, try using different coloured wool. When you are really good, try different patterns, such as the ones on the previous page.
- The most important thing is to EXPERIMENT and HAVE FUN.

## Try the diamond design

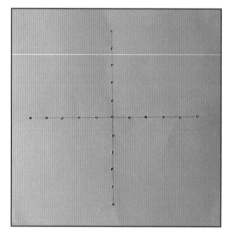

Start

*The more holes you make the bigger the pattern will be...*

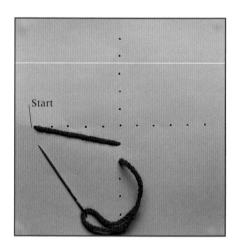

# 1 Get weaving

Now for the fun bit: weave your woolly webs.

Start by threading the wool up through the FIRST hole along the bottom, and down through the SECOND hole up the side.

# 2

Now bring the wool up through the THIRD hole up, as shown, and down through the SECOND hole along.

# 3

Now up through the THIRD hole along and down through the FOURTH hole up. Get the picture?

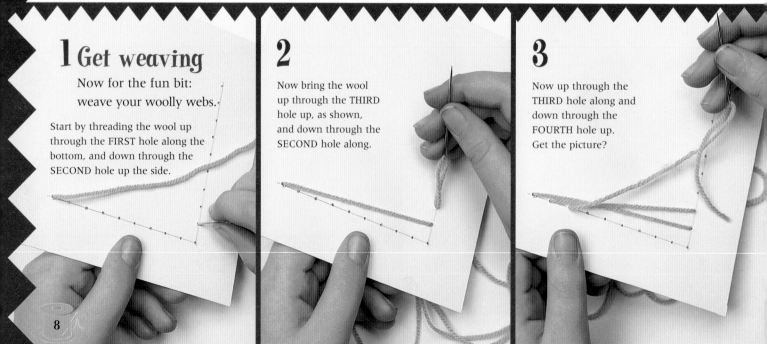

Mark dots along your lines, one every centimetre (half inch). You should end up with a row of 10 dots along and 10 dots up.

With a darning needle, make a hole through each dot.

Place some thick card underneath to protect the table.

Now thread some wool onto the needle and knot the end.

## 2 Mark out the dots

## 3 Make your holes

## 4 Thread a needle

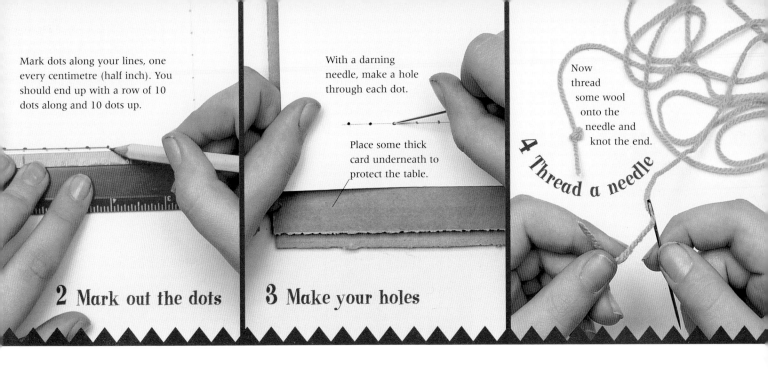

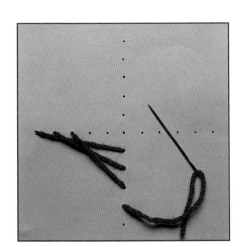 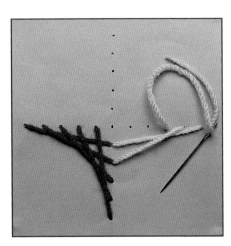 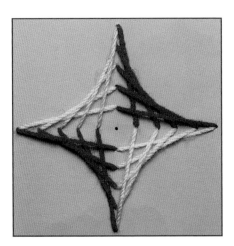

**and remember, you can use each hole more than once. Go on, weave a giant web!**

### 4
Carry on weaving in this pattern until you have no more holes to fill.

### 5
The last hole you use should be the top one, so thread down through it and stop.

### 6
Turn the card over, tie a knot as close to the last stitch as possible, and trim the end of the wool.

## The ABC of cross-stitch

When you've perfected your A, B, Cs, put your letters together to make a name, write a message, or even draw a cross-stitch picture.

# Cross-stitch

**Simple samplers** are as easy as A, B, C. Criss, cross, criss, cross, and create pictures.

# Following guide lines

• Draw out the area you want to sew as small squares – each square is one cross-stitch.
• To keep your letters the same size, base them on the same number of squares across and up – for example, 4 squares across and 7 squares up.
• Remember, the curving part of a letter still has to be drawn using the squares.

Don't make the line too dark or it will show through your stitches.

*Pencil*

*Binca fabric*        *Darning needle*

## You will need

BINCA FABRIC • The large holes make it easy to see where to sew.

THREAD • Use anything from fine silk thread to thick wool.

NEEDLE • A darning needle is easy to thread and fits through the holes.

PENCIL • To mark out the squares.

*Embroidery thread*

*Scissors*

## Single stitch

For one stitch use a short length of thread and don't forget to knot the end.

## Stitches in a row

To make a row, sew a few stitches, then go back the other way.

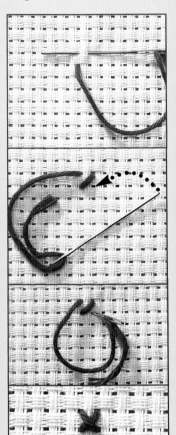

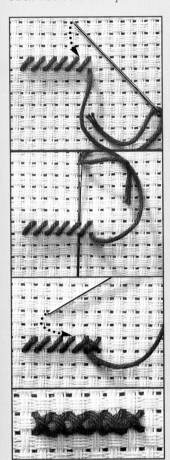

## Back view and finishing off

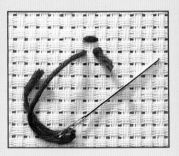

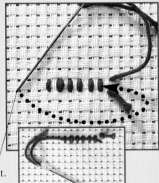

Finish a stitch on the back and thread it through other nearby stitches to secure it.

## A·B·C cross-stitch letter squares

Once you have learnt how to cross-stitch, experiment with different patterns and colours. To start, try these single letters. Cut a square of fabric about 18 holes by 18 holes. Draw on your design in pencil, and stitch away.

Try fringing the edges of your work by pulling away the first few strands of the fabric along the edge.

13

# Pirate Pete

**Yo, ho, ho, it's a pirate's life for me!** How would you like to be drawn, sewn, and stuffed? That's how I'm made.

Ship a'hoy!

## Shiver me beanbags

This jolly pirate is stuffed full of rice. You can use dried food, such as lentils, popping corn, dried beans, or small pasta. Don't stuff it too full, however – it needs to be a bit floppy.

## Follow the lines and dots

The hard line shows you where you cut the material, and the dotted line shows you where you sew.

Include these ears for cat shape.

Leave a space here to fill your toy.

TRACING PAPER

PEN

SCISSORS

# Pirate pattern

Sew along this line.

Cut out along this line.

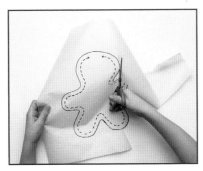

Snip away these triangles from the material. This will help the shape to turn inside out neatly.

Place a piece of tracing paper over this page and draw around the outline you have chosen. Cut the shape out.

Cut straight along here for ghost or snowman shapes.

# Meet the gang

**"All aboard the Jolly Roger!"**
shouts Pete. He couldn't sail his ship
without his trusted beanbag crew.
"Hoist the sails, raise
the anchor,
we're off to find
hidden treasure!"

### Beanbag tips

Pete's pattern can be
used to make the crew
too. Just add extra ears
for the animals, woolly plaits for
the girls, and leave out the legs
for the ghosts and snowman.

Whoo
hoooo

16

I'm off to sail the seven seas

Moo-ieoow!

# Throw together Pete

## Pirate Pete is ready to be cut out

for a life on the high seas. Use the template from page 15 to make him and go on to throw together his whole crew. "Ha, ha, me hearties!"

### YOUR PIRATE KIT

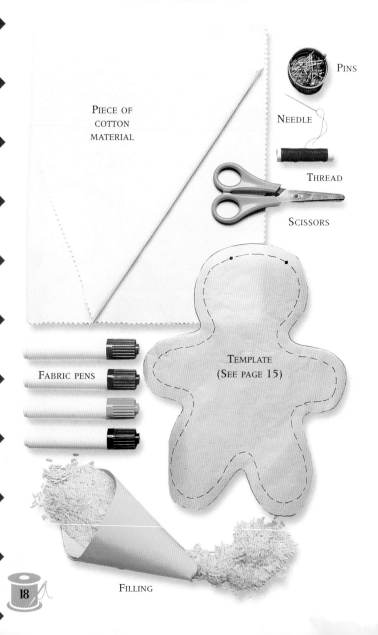

PINS

NEEDLE

THREAD

SCISSORS

PIECE OF COTTON MATERIAL

FABRIC PENS

TEMPLATE (SEE PAGE 15)

FILLING

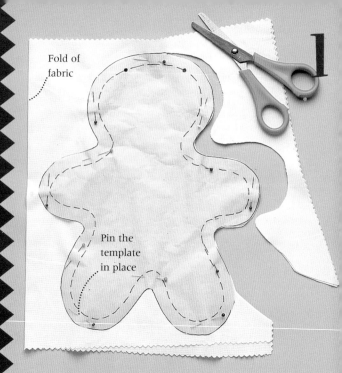

Fold of fabric

Pin the template in place

**1**

## Cut out the shape

Fold a piece of material in half. Lay your template on top. Cut it out. You will now have two Pete shapes.

Leave a gap so you have room to fill him.

**4**

Cut out the diamond shapes shown on the template. This makes it easier to turn Pete inside out.

## Sew all the way around

Use small backstitches (see page 5) to sew around the pirate. Leave a small gap at the top.

Use fabric pens to colour Pirate Pete.

**2**

## Draw Pirate Pete

Colour the front of Pete on one piece and draw the back of him on the other.

**3**

## Pin the pieces together

Place the right sides of Pete together and pin them in place.

Turn the fabric through the gap in the stitching.

**5**

## Turn him inside out

You should now see the right sides of Pete on the outside.

Curl a piece of paper into a tube funnel for easy filling.

When you have filled Pete, fold the open edges inwards, pin them together, and stitch the opening.

**6**

## Fill him up

Fill up Pirate Pete with rice or beans, and sew him up!

# Knitted pals

## Short of soft toys?

Ted sits and knits a pal or two to play with him – and so could you!

Bobble hat

Hold on to your hats!

## Easy knitting

Once you get the hang of knitting, you can make lots of different things. All the knitted projects in this book are made from squares and rectangles only – this makes them really easy! Start off with Ted, move onto his pals, then knit them all scarves and bobble hats.

Off we go...

# How to get started

## YOU WILL NEED...

KNITTING NEEDLES SIZE 4 MM (NO 8)

## Casting on
This is how you get the stitches onto the needle. The pattern will tell you how many to cast on.

| | | | |
|---|---|---|---|
| Tie the wool onto the needle, then pick up the wool and loop it once. | Now twist the loop again. | Slip the loop onto the needle. | Pull the wool so it is quite tight. |

## Knitting stitches
Follow these instructions and just keep knitting and knitting and knitting!

### Through the loop...
We are using different coloured needles to make it easier for instruction. Tuck the yellow needle through the first loop – it should lie behind the red one.

### Wind around...
Wrap the trailing wool around the yellow needle from right to left.

## Casting off
When you have have done enough rows, finish your knitting by "casting off".

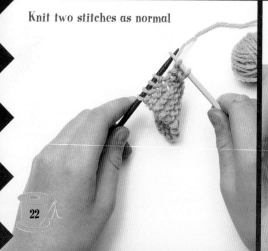

Knit two stitches as normal

On the yellow needle, take hold of the first stitch.

Pull the stitch right over the second and off the needle.

Knit another stitch and do the same again.

SCISSORS

WOOL

# Row counter

This is a handy gadget that slides on to a needle. Each time you finish a row turn the the dial to show the number you have done.

ROW COUNTER

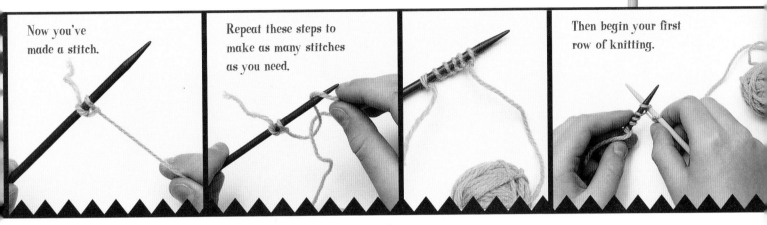

Now you've made a stitch.

Repeat these steps to make as many stitches as you need.

Then begin your first row of knitting.

**Under it goes...** Bring the yellow needle back up to the front with the loop still attached.

**Off it comes** Slip the stitch off the red needle, keeping it on the yellow one.

Carry on until you have one stitch left.

Snip the wool.

Bring the end of the wool through the loop and pull tight. This will secure it.

# Making Ted
Knit five pieces, sew them up, stuff them, and join them together. Hello Ted!

## 1

Knit these five body pieces with the number of rows and stitches shown.

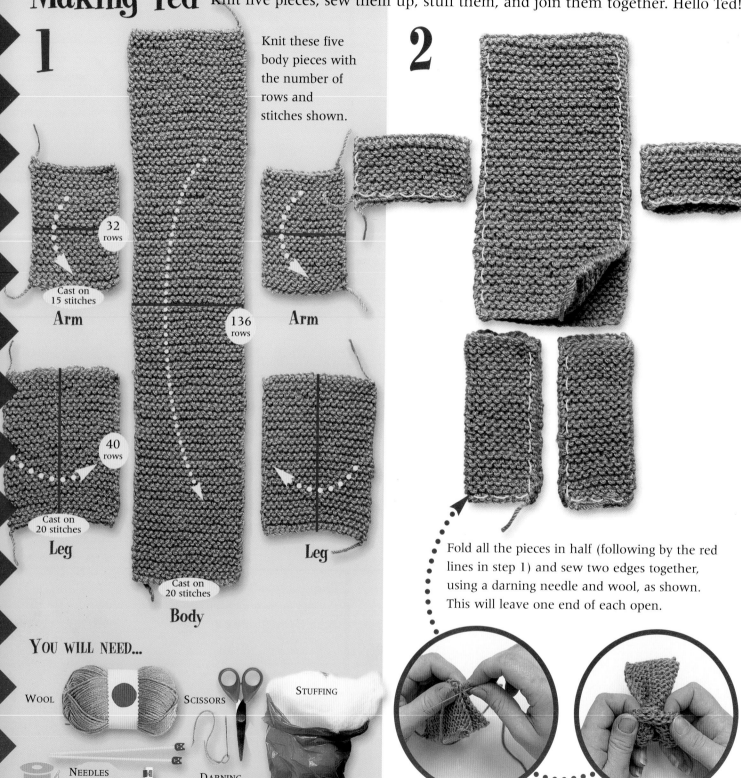

**Arm**
32 rows
Cast on 15 stitches

**Arm**

**Leg**
40 rows
Cast on 20 stitches

**Body**
136 rows
Cast on 20 stitches

**Leg**

### YOU WILL NEED...

WOOL   SCISSORS   STUFFING

NEEDLES   DARNING NEEDLE
ROW COUNTER

24

## 2

Fold all the pieces in half (following by the red lines in step 1) and sew two edges together, using a darning needle and wool, as shown. This will leave one end of each open.

Watch me jump

## 3

Turn each piece inside out and stuff them. Sew up the end of each knitted piece.

## 4

Now sew the arms and legs to the body. Make sure you put them in the right place. You don't want a wonky Ted!

Use buttons for my eyes and nose.

Tie a bow under my chin to give me a neck.

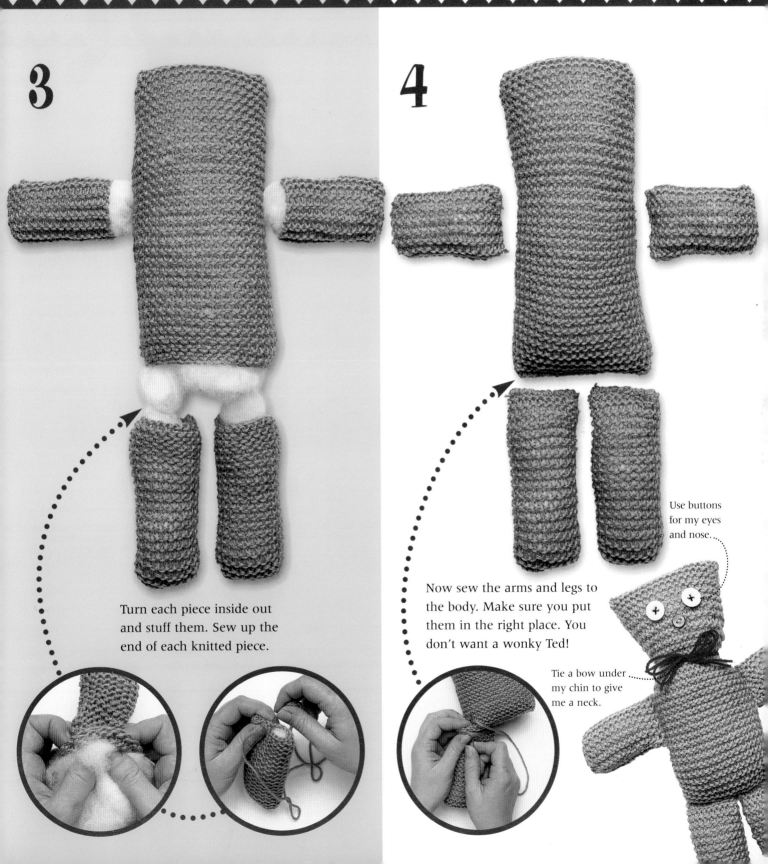

# Ted's friends

## You can't just make Ted, you need to make Ted's friends too. And what happens if they get cold? Knit them scarves and bobble hats of course!

## Make a friend for Ted

Ted's friend is very easy because he has wibbly-wobbly arms and legs.

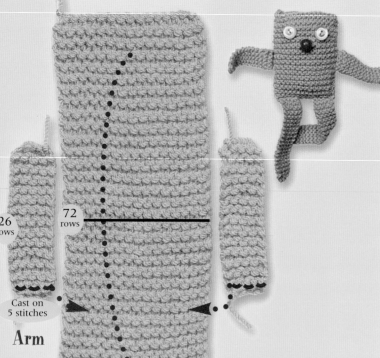

26 rows

72 rows

Cast on 5 stitches

**Arm**

**Body**

Cast on 16 stitches

40 rows

**Leg**

Cast on 5 stitches

## Making friends

Knit the five body pieces, as shown. Fold the body in half, sew up two sides, turn it inside out, and stuff it – just like you did with Ted. Then sew up the body and attach the arms and legs.

## Beanie hats

Everyone needs a hat.

## Hat making

Ted's friend wants a hat. To make one, cast on 54 stitches and knit 20 rows. Fold in half, as above, and sew the top and sides together. Pop it on and turn up the bottom.

Sew on old buttons or beads for the eyes and nose.

# A pom-pom for the hat

Cut out two discs from thin card. Cut a hole in the middle of each one.

5 cm (2 in) across

Put the discs together and tie a piece of wool around them.

Wind the wool around and around through the middle and over the top. Stop when the discs are covered.

Use different colours.

Put a pair of scissors between the discs and snip the wool all around.

Tie a piece of wool tightly around the pom-pom.

Take away the card discs and fluff it up!

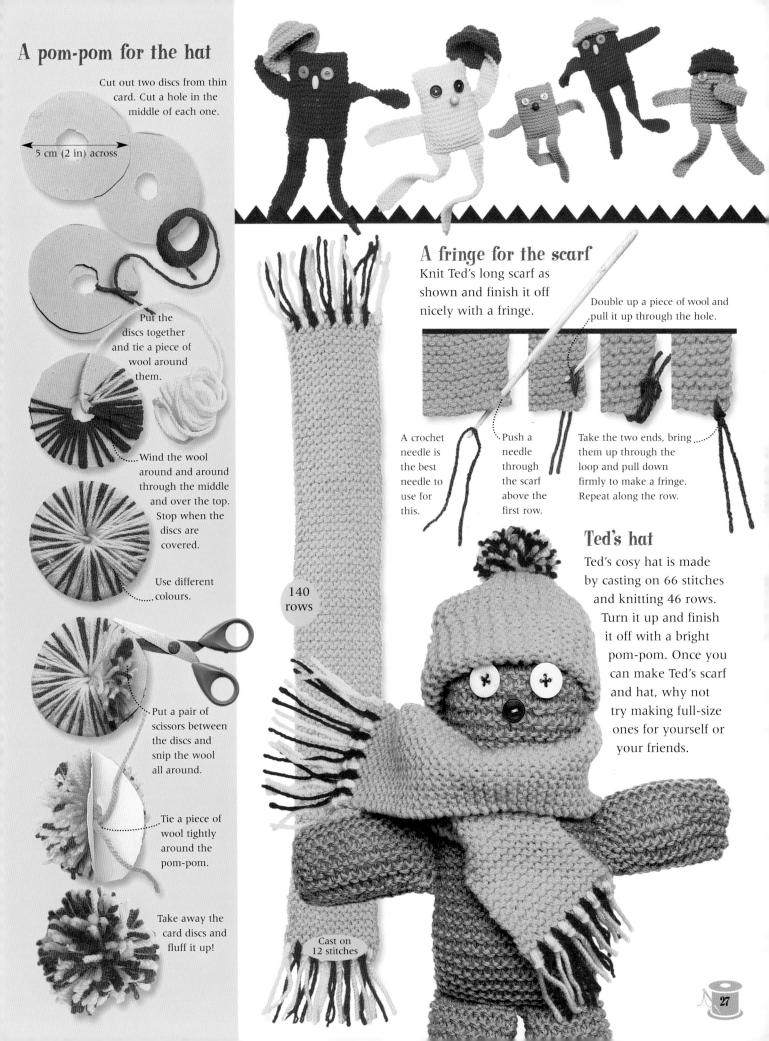

## A fringe for the scarf

Knit Ted's long scarf as shown and finish it off nicely with a fringe.

Double up a piece of wool and pull it up through the hole.

A crochet needle is the best needle to use for this.

Push a needle through the scarf above the first row.

Take the two ends, bring them up through the loop and pull down firmly to make a fringe. Repeat along the row.

140 rows

Cast on 12 stitches

## Ted's hat

Ted's cosy hat is made by casting on 66 stitches and knitting 46 rows. Turn it up and finish it off with a bright pom-pom. Once you can make Ted's scarf and hat, why not try making full-size ones for yourself or your friends.

# Marble paper

It's so good, the technique
needs to be kept a secret!

# Special effects

Marble paper looks so good
it will astound your friends,
AND it's really easy to do.
Once you have made it, you
can wrap things in it, cover
things with it, use it as a
frame, or write on it.
You'll impress everyone
you know!

# The marble effect

## Oil and water don't mix – that's why
the paint stays on the surface of the water – and
that's how it makes wiggly, marbly swirls on the
paper. If it doesn't make sense, don't worry, just
follow the instructions – you'll be amazed.

# The paint mixture

Before you start, make some pots of paint
mixture in different colours. Squeeze a
blob of oil paint into a pot and add four
caps full of turpentine. Mix them
together. The paint will become very thin.

⭐ **Ask an adult** to help mix the
paint with turpentine.

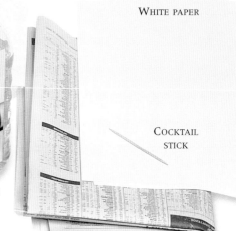

KITCHEN
TOWEL

WHITE PAPER

COCKTAIL
STICK

PAINT
POTS

TURPENTINE

NEWSPAPER

BAKING TRAY
WITH WATER

OIL PAINTS

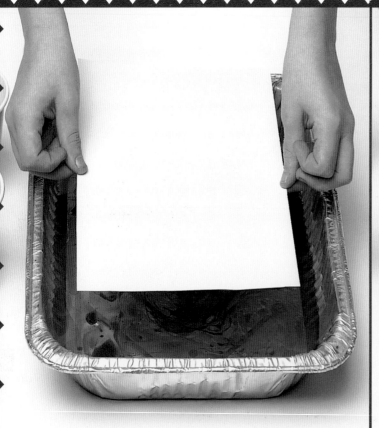

## 3 Lay the paper on it
Just let the paper float on to the water.

## 4 Give it a prod
Gently push the paper to help it make contact.

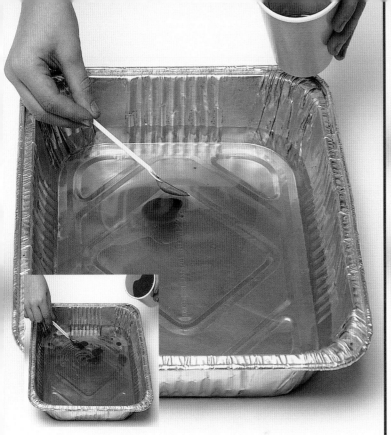

## 1 Add the paint to some water

Pour about 3 cm (1 in) of water into the tray. Add small spoonfuls of each colour paint mixture.

## 2 Swirl the paint around

With a cocktail stick, swirl the paint gently in the water, but don't mix it too well

## 5 Remove the paper

Pick up the corners and lift the paper out quickly.

## 6 Leave it to dry

Allow it to dry flat on newspaper.

# Printing patterns

**Take plain or coloured paper** and transform it into a frenzy of pattern. Go on, get printing!

# Making patterns

## YOU WILL NEED...

PAPER • Lots of paper to print on, such as brown packing paper, large sheets of plain white paper, or coloured paper.

PAINT • The best paint to use is poster paint but any paint you have will do.

Try these babies' footprints using your hand – you could even use your own feet.

## Babies' footprints

Dip the side of your fist into some paint.

Make a print on the paper.

Use your fingertips for the toes.

# Odds and ends

Search around the house for any items that you think would be good for printing. Remember to ask if you can cover them in paint first! Then dip them in the paint and press down on the paper.

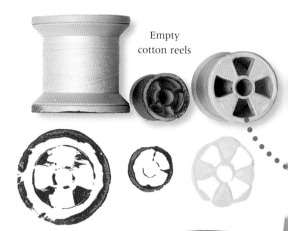

Empty cotton reels

Pen end

Scrunched up plastic or paper bag

Sponge

Cake cutters

Dip the reels into the paint.

Press down onto the paper.

Plastic letters

Carved-out carrot

Bubble wrap

Carved-out potato

Pen end

Brush

# A star box

Stuff your star full of sweets and other delicious little fancies.

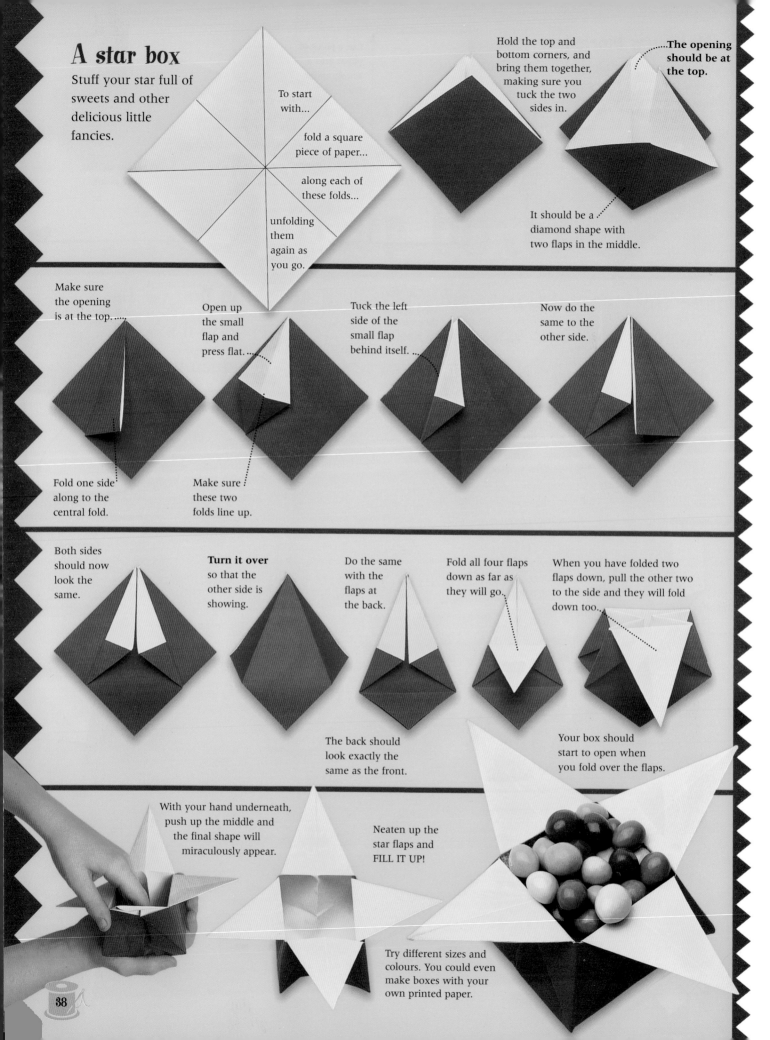

To start with... fold a square piece of paper... along each of these folds... unfolding them again as you go.

Hold the top and bottom corners, and bring them together, making sure you tuck the two sides in.

**The opening should be at the top.**

It should be a diamond shape with two flaps in the middle.

Make sure the opening is at the top.....

Open up the small flap and press flat. ....

Tuck the left side of the small flap behind itself. ....

Now do the same to the other side.

Fold one side along to the central fold.

Make sure these two folds line up.

Both sides should now look the same.

**Turn it over** so that the other side is showing.

Do the same with the flaps at the back.

Fold all four flaps down as far as they will go.

When you have folded two flaps down, pull the other two to the side and they will fold down too...

The back should look exactly the same as the front.

Your box should start to open when you fold over the flaps.

With your hand underneath, push up the middle and the final shape will miraculously appear.

Neaten up the star flaps and FILL IT UP!

Try different sizes and colours. You could even make boxes with your own printed paper.

38

# A galaxy of star boxes

## Star gifts

This box design makes a
fantastic container for gifts.
Try making it with comics
and wrapping
paper too.

## Fold-up box

For this simple box,
fold a rectangular piece
of paper in half and half
again along the length,
then unfold it. Now
you have some useful
folds to work with.

Fold in two
ends so they
meet in the
middle.

Tuck down all
four corners,
as shown, but
not quite to
the middle.

Fold back
one central
flap to the
edge of the
corner folds.

Fold back
the other
central flap.

Take hold of the
two side folds in
the centre and
pull them apart.

Neaten up the
shape and there
you have it –
a quick and
easy box.

**Fill it up
with goodies**

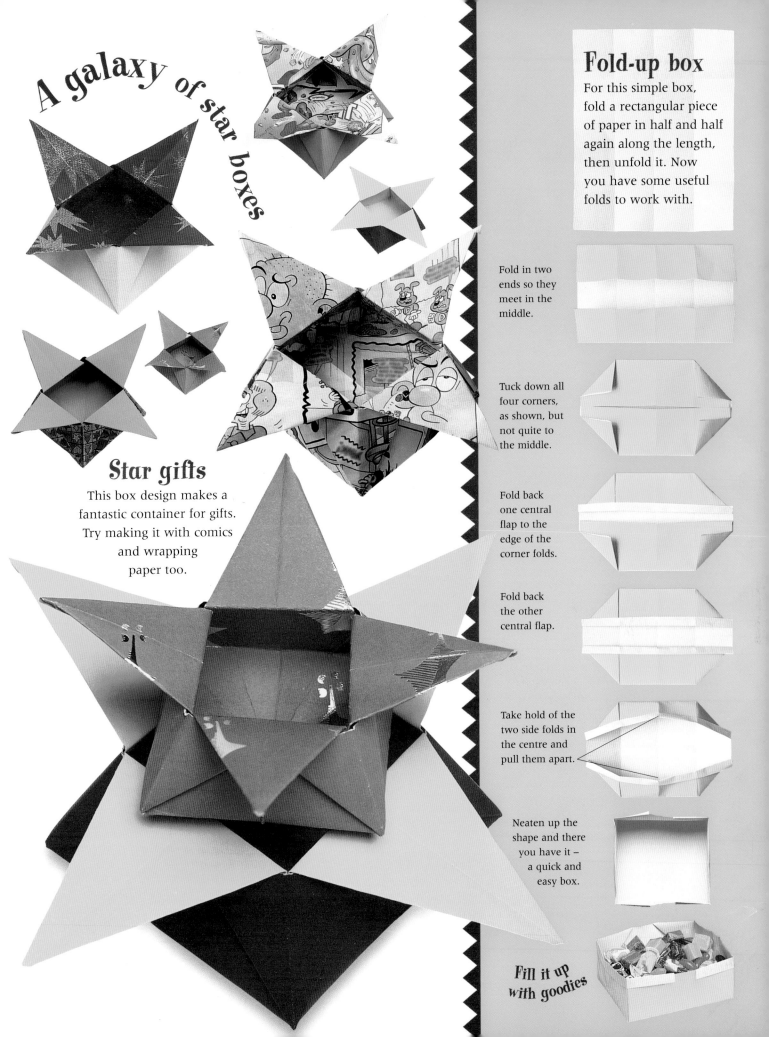

# Paper roses

**Fill a vase** with home-grown tissue flowers and give a bunch to your mum.

## Wild roses

Create a really wild, colourful bouquet by mixing and matching colours. If you want to make rose trees, turn the page for instructions.

# To make a rose

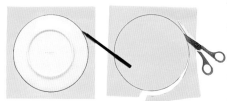

Place a plate, about 15 cm (6 in) wide on a piece of tissue paper.

Draw around it and cut the circle. Repeat until you have six discs.

Place the discs on top of each other.

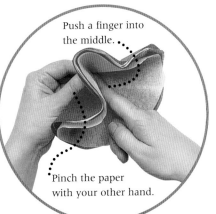

Push a finger into the middle.

Pinch the paper with your other hand.

Squeeze the bottom of the paper tightly.

Tape the paper to a straw "stem".

# Rose trees

# Rows of roses

SMALL PLATE

TISSUE PAPER

STICKY TAPE

PEN

SCISSORS

DRINKING STRAWS

## Perfect petals

Finally, pull the layers apart carefully to fluff up the flower.

**2** Now glue the other end of the zig-zag.

**3** Close the card.

**1** Stick it down on one side.

**4** Both sides should now be stuck on the inside so when you open it the tutu will pop up.

**Concertina ballerina**
Take a strip of card and fold it into a zig-zag as shown in step 1. Then glue one end.

**5**

## Concertina cards

It's always great to get a card, especially if it's home-made. For someone really special try making a 3-D card! Create the concertina ballerina.

# Crafty cards
Using all the crafty ideas in this book.

### Comic card

Fold up a comic page and snip a few holes out of it, open it up, and stick it on a card!

### Woolly web card

Your woolly webs are perfect patterns to stick onto cards.

### Cross-stitch A B C

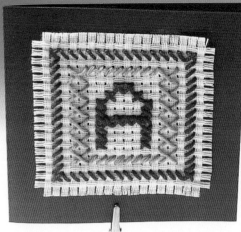

Use the initial of the person you are sending the card to and cross-stitch it.

### Parcel tags

Home-made tags finish off a present perfectly. Cut a tag shape out of card, make a hole in the end, and tie a ribbon through it. Write on the card or decorate it first.

### Giving gifts

The tissue-paper roses on the previous page make lovely gifts. Pop one into a vase or turn several into a rose tree by putting them into a plastic cup. To do this, place a piece of sticky tack in the bottom of the cup and firmly push the straw stalk into it. Decorate the outside and give it as a present.

Three paper roses

Green tissue paper

Glue a piece of tissue paper around the cup and snip the edges.

### Paper roses

The paper roses can also be stuck flat on a card or tag.

# Special delivery

## Cards and envelopes can be made from your own printed paper – or any paper you choose.

Aunty Daisy
The Rose Garden
Buddley Petalton

## Home-made envelopes

When you have made your cards, sometimes it's difficult to find the perfect-sized envelope to fit them. Your best bet is to make one yourself. You can even make it to match your card.

Measure your card to check that it will fit in the envelope.

Take a square piece of card and fold the left and right corners into the middle.

Fold the bottom corner up to the middle.

Fold the top flap down last, and when you have put a card inside, use a sticker to seal it.

To **Mum**

Dad

Grandma
Knitted Cottage
woolly Hatbury

Make envelopes out of
magazines, comics, wrapping
paper, or even brown paper.

For an even
simpler envelope, take a
rectangular piece of card
and fold it into three
sections.

Unfold it and glue
the edges of the
bottom
section.

Fold the top flap down.

Use a sticker to seal
the envelope down.

Write your
addresses on
sticky labels.

# It's a wrap!

## All wrapped up.

Give away your crafty projects as presents, wrapped in home-made paper with matching name tags.

## Tags

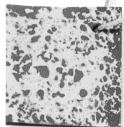

Cut a shape out of heavy paper or card and make a hole in the corner.

Tie a piece of ribbon or wool through the hole.

## Wrap it up

Take a piece of your home-made paper, and put the present in the middle.

Fold one side over the top and hold it in place.

Fold the other side over and tape in place.

Push the centre of the paper down firmly.

Pull one side in and hold it in place.

You could write a note on the tag...

To Mum

or print a pattern on it.

Fold the other side in.

Fold up the triangle shape and tape in place.

To match a tag to the footprint paper cut around the print, make a hole, and tie some wool through it.

## The personal touch

Now you have a gift all wrapped up in your home-made, personalised wrapping paper.

Thanks Ted! Are these all from you?

# Index

# Acknowledgements

With thanks to...
Eleanor Bates, Charlotte Bull,
Billy Bull, and James Bull for
craftily performing the arty
projects.

All images © Dorling Kindersley.
For further information see:
www.dkimages.com

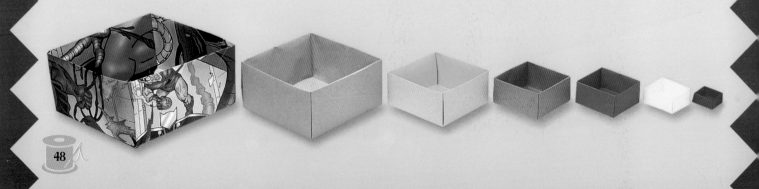